SCHOLASTIC

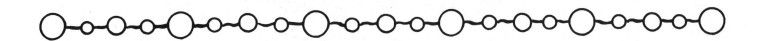

Independent
READING RESPONSE
Booklets

by Karen Kellaher

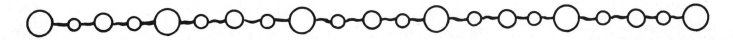

New York • Toronto • London • Auckland • Sydney
Mexico City • New Delhi • Hong Kong • Buenos Aires

Teaching *Resources*

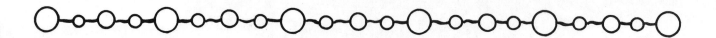

Dedication
To Mo Bear
with love.

Cover design by Josué Castilleja

Interior design by Ellen Matlach for Boultinghouse & Boultinghouse, Inc.

Cover and interior illustrations by Teresa Anderko

ISBN: 0-439-39513-5

Copyright © 2004 by Karen Kellaher

Published by Scholastic Inc.

4 5 6 7 8 9 10   40   11 10 09 08 07 06 05

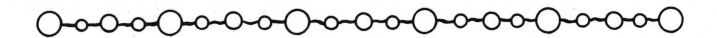

Contents

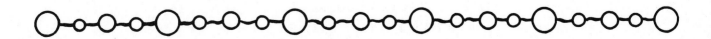

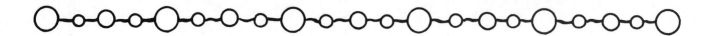

Introduction

Welcome to *Independent Reading Response Booklets*—an instant and engaging way for students to respond to any fiction or nonfiction book! Each of the 15 reproducible booklets is full of creative writing prompts that guide students to reflect on what they've read. Students will enjoy the variety of booklets, each with its own fun and unique approach, such as an advice column, a reporter's notebook, a character scrapbook, and a newspaper. In the process, they'll explore character, setting, conflict and resolution, point of view, main idea and details, visual aids, and more. These booklets help students accomplish the following:

Respond to both fiction and nonfiction.
You'll find eight booklets for fiction that focus on literary elements and seven booklets that highlight the elements of nonfiction.

Boost reading comprehension.
The writing prompts encourage students to respond thoughtfully to the text and provide examples to support their ideas.

Engage in meaningful writing.
Students write about important and interesting aspects of the books they've read to create their own personalized booklets.

Connections to the Language Arts Standards
These booklets help students meet the following language arts standards outlined by Mid-continent Research for Education and Learning (McREL), a nationally recognized nonprofit organization that collects and synthesizes national and state K–12 standards.

Uses the general skills and strategies of the writing process
• Writes in response to literature (e.g., summarizes main ideas and significant details; relates own ideas to supporting details; advances judgments; supports judgments with references to the text)

Uses reading skills and strategies to understand and interpret a variety of literary texts
• Uses reading skills and strategies to understand a variety of literary passages and texts (e.g., fairy tales, folktales, fiction, nonfiction, myths, poems, fables, fantasies, historical fiction, biographies, autobiographies, chapter books)
• Understands the basic concept of plot (e.g., main problem, conflict, resolution, cause and effect)
• Understands elements of character development in literary works (e.g., the importance of a character's actions, motives, and appearance to plot and theme)

Uses reading skills and strategies to understand and interpret a variety of informational texts
• Understands the main idea and supporting details of simple expository information
• Summarizes information found in texts (e.g., retells in own words)
• Summarizes and paraphrases information in texts (e.g., includes the main idea and significant supporting details of a reading selection)
• Uses prior knowledge and experience to understand and respond to new information

Source: *Content Knowledge: A Compendium of Standards and Benchmarks for K–12 Education,* 4th edition (Mid-continent Research for Education and Learning)

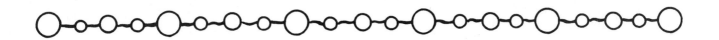

How to Use This Book

You can incorporate these booklets into any independent reading program and use them in a number of ways. The following are suggested guidelines.

Getting Started

The first eight booklets were designed for responding to fictional books and the remaining seven for nonfiction books. They work for a variety of text levels, from picture books to chapter books. Students can use these booklets to respond to independent reading or to a book you've read together as a class.

In advance, review the teaching notes for each booklet on pages 6–10. Before students begin working on a booklet, review the directions on each page with them. If students need additional guidance, complete a booklet together based on a book you've read as a class. You might have students work on the same booklet or different booklets. You can also assign the same booklet for different books throughout the year. Once students are familiar with the booklets, you might have them choose which booklet they would like to complete. To guide students' selections, store the booklets in folders labeled "fiction" or "nonfiction" along with the names of the booklets.

Meeting Students' Needs

These booklets were designed for independent use. Based on students' needs, you might assign parts of a booklet rather than all of it, or you might have them complete a few pages at a time. For an additional challenge, use one or more of the prompts as the basis for a longer writing assignment.

Assessing Students' Work

The prompts in these booklets move beyond factual questions so that students truly reflect on what they've read. They encourage students to develop their own ideas about the material and to support their ideas with evidence from the text. In addition, the creative nature of the booklets motivates children to personalize their work with their own creative flair.

Reading-response booklets provide a window into what students are learning, thinking, feeling, and wondering about their independent reading. The completed booklets can be used for assessment of both reading comprehension and writing skills. Collect the booklets and provide constructive feedback on the thoroughness and thoughtfulness of students' responses. If students are completing one section at a time, you might respond to each section as they complete it, or you might respond to the whole booklet once they have finished. The booklets also provide a helpful starting place for book conferences with students. If time allows, invite students to share favorite sections of their booklets with small groups or the whole class (remind them not to give away the endings of their books). Completed booklets also make a nice addition to students' writing portfolios.

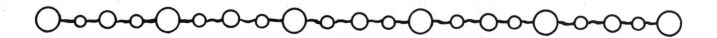

Making and Using the Booklets

Follow the instructions for photocopying each booklet. Then demonstrate the assembly directions for students so they can put together their own booklets. Most of the booklets are designed for double-sided copying. If your copier has a double-sided function, carefully remove the perforated booklet pages and make double-sided copies.

If your copier does not have a double-sided function, make single-sided copies of the first page. Place these copies in the paper tray and make copies of the second page so that it appears on the back of the first page. Check to be sure that the pages are copying exactly as they appear in the book (for example, with booklet page 1 appearing directly behind the cover). You may need to experiment with the placement of pages in the paper tray and the direction of pages to be copied. Follow the same steps with any remaining pages, again checking that pages are copying as they appear in the book.

When folding the pages, fold carefully along the dotted lines. Fold the first page so that the cover appears on the outside. Fold the second page so that booklet page 2 appears on the outside.

Imagine That...

pages 11–14 • Fiction

Point out that the booklet is shaped like a thought balloon to emphasize that students should use their imagination to answer the questions. Explain that students should use information from their books to answer the booklet questions creatively. Remind students that many of the questions ask them to explain their answers.

Assembly: Make double-sided copies of the booklet pages. Fold each page in half along the dotted line and nest the pages in numerical order. Cut out the shape and staple along the top edge.

A Writing "Ad"venture

pages 15–16 • Fiction

In this booklet, students will create small ads that look like those in the yellow pages. They will choose products or services that could help a particular character solve a problem. Read aloud the text on the cover and ask students to name a few kinds of products and services. Then show them advertisements from the yellow pages, as well as from newspapers or magazines. Ask students to describe the features of an ad (such as persuasive text and illustrations or photos). Review the directions together and brainstorm examples of products that could help well-known characters. For example, Cinderella could use a reliable wristwatch to help her return from the ball on time. Encourage students to refer to the sample advertisements for inspiration as they are writing.

Assembly: Make double-sided copies of the booklet pages. Fold the page in half along the dotted line.

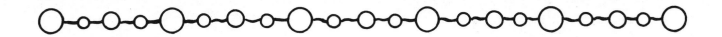

My Advice Column
pages 17–18 • Fiction

In this booklet, students will write short letters from characters describing a problem they are having. Then they'll respond as an advice columnist with some helpful words of wisdom. Share an age-appropriate advice column with children. (If you can't find one, write a short, imaginary letter and response.) Explain that people sometimes use pen names when signing off because they don't want to reveal their identities. Review the directions with students and provide some examples of problems and solutions. You might assign this booklet while students are still reading the book, so they won't know how the characters' problems are solved. If students have completed the book, ask them to think of alternate solutions to the problems. Invite students to make up fun pen names for their characters to use in signing off (for example, "Nervous in Nevada").

Assembly: Make double-sided copies of the booklet pages. Cut the page in half along the solid line. Place the pages in numerical order and fold along the dotted line. Staple along the left edge.

Character Scrapbook
pages 19–22 • Fiction

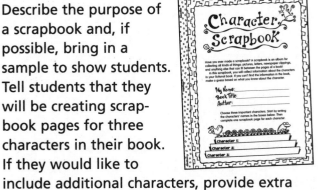

Describe the purpose of a scrapbook and, if possible, bring in a sample to show students. Tell students that they will be creating scrapbook pages for three characters in their book. If they would like to include additional characters, provide extra copies of booklet pages 1–3. Review the writing and drawing prompts on each page. Explain that for favorite quotation, students should choose something that the character said that they enjoyed or thought was important. If students need additional guidance, make an overhead transparency of one of the scrapbook pages. Then fill it in together with information about a character from a book you've read as a class.

Assembly: Make single-sided copies of the booklet pages. Have students complete the pages before stapling them together along the left side.

How I See It
pages 23–26 • Fiction

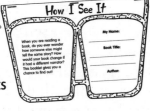

This booklet illustrates the concept of point of view and guides students to imagine how their book would change if there were a different narrator. This assignment works especially well with stories that have a central conflict or disagreement because it's interesting to imagine how each character would tell the tale from his or her perspective.

Before beginning, discuss the factors that contribute to point of view (past experiences, character traits and opinions, and so on). Then talk about the two kinds of narrators described on booklet page 1. If possible, show an example of a book with each kind of narrator. If point of view is a new concept for students, choose a book that you've read as a class or read aloud a picture book to students. Work together to choose an event and summarize it from the perspectives of different characters. Then fill in the booklet together. If students need extra support, have them tell you the event and characters that they chose before they begin writing. Or have students choose only one new narrator.

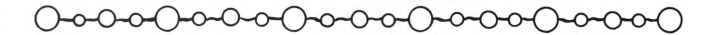

Assembly: Make double-sided copies of the booklet pages. Fold each page in half along the dotted line and nest the pages in numerical order. Cut out the shape and staple along the top edge.

My Book of Lists for Fiction

pages 27–29 • Fiction

In this booklet, students will make lists of items that relate to their book—five new words, four interesting characters, three favorite parts, two important places, and one book review. Invite students to use the blank reverse sides of the booklet pages to add illustrations.

Assembly: Make single-sided copies of the booklet pages. Cut along the solid lines to create six booklet pages of different heights. Stack the pages on top of each other in order by size, as shown. Place the longest page on the bottom and the shortest page (the cover) on top. Align the pages along the top edge and staple them together.

Reporter's Notebook

pages 30–32 • Fiction

Ask students what they think a reporter would use a notebook for. What might the reporter record in it? Explain that students will have a chance to pretend they are reporting on the book they've just read. They'll even get a notebook to record their observations. Review the questions answered in a news article: Who? What? Where?

When? How? and Why? Tell students that they will answer one of these questions on each page of their notebooks. Once students have completed their booklets, you might have them write a full news story based on one important event in their book.

Assembly: Make single-sided copies of the booklet pages. Have students cut along the solid lines to create six elongated booklet pages. Arrange the pages in numerical order and staple along the top edge.

The Envelope, Please...

pages 33–37 • Fiction

This booklet gives students the chance to nominate certain aspects of their books for an award,

name a winner, and explain their selection. Point out that this booklet is based on an awards ceremony, such as those shown on television for actors. Describe the proceedings of an awards ceremony. You might assign students all of the awards or select a few. The last award template is blank so that students may create their own award category.

Assembly: For each booklet, you will need five plain business-size envelopes. Place each envelope with the flap facing you, open the flap, and cut off the right corner of the flap, as shown. This will make the flaps easier to open once the booklet is assembled. Stack the envelopes with the flaps facing down and staple along the left side.

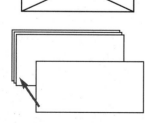

Make single-sided copies of the booklet pages and cut out all the boxes. Some boxes will be glued onto the envelopes and others

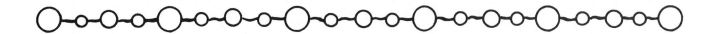

will be folded and inserted into the envelopes, as follows:

Envelope 1:

- Glue page 1A onto the front of the envelope.
- Close the flap and glue page 1B onto the back.

Envelope 2:

- Glue page 2A onto the front of the envelope.
- Fold page 2B and place inside.
- Glue a box with the text "And the award goes to…" onto the back.

(Follow the same steps for envelopes 3–5.)

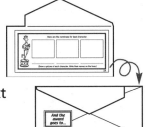

My Book of Lists for Nonfiction

pages 38–40 • Nonfiction

In this booklet, students will make lists of items that relate to their book—five new words, four interesting facts, three helpful visual aids, two questions about the topic, and one book review. Invite students to use the blank reverse sides of the booklet pages to add illustrations.

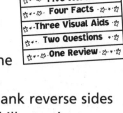

Assembly: Make single-sided copies of the booklet pages. Cut along the solid lines to create six booklet pages of different heights. Stack the pages on top of each other in order by size, as shown. Place the longest page on the bottom and the shortest page (the cover) on top. Align the pages along the top edge and staple them together.

Reader's Report Card

pages 41–44 • Nonfiction

In this booklet, students grade their nonfiction books on interest level, organization, visual aids, writing style, and information. Instruct students to provide explanations for each grade they assign and include specific examples from the text. If students have read the same book, have them work in small groups to compare their evaluations.

Assembly: Make double-sided copies of the booklet pages. Fold each page in half along the dotted line and nest the pages in numerical order. Staple along the left edge.

Up, Up, and Away With Nonfiction!

pages 45–48 • Nonfiction

In this booklet, students answer a variety of questions about their books—from recalling their favorite part to brainstorming a new title and cover. To introduce the booklet, discuss the idea that reading a nonfiction book is like taking a trip: you see new sights, meet new people, and learn lots of interesting things. Encourage students to think about all the things they learned in their book.

Assembly: Make double-sided copies of the booklet pages. Fold each page in half along the dotted line and nest the pages in numerical order. Cut out the shape and staple along the left edge.

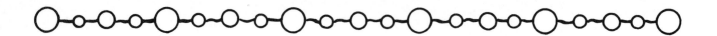

Read to Learn!

pages 49–52 • Nonfiction

In this booklet, students explore several elements of nonfiction. Read the directions on each page together and provide examples of responses. You might have students work on this booklet while they are reading their books so they can be on the lookout for examples to include.

Assembly: Make double-sided copies of the booklet pages. Fold each page in half along the dotted line and nest the pages in numerical order. Cut out the shape and staple along the left side.

Postcards From _____

pages 53–56 • Nonfiction

This booklet is a collection of three postcards that students write and illustrate about three important things in their book—a person (or animal), a place, and an object. Encourage students to describe each and explain its importance in the book. Show students several postcards for inspiration.

Assembly: Make double-sided copies of the booklet pages. Cut along the solid lines, arrange in numerical order, and staple along the left side.

Nonfiction Newspaper

pages 57–60 • Nonfiction

Introduce and assign one section of this booklet at a time. Show students the different sections of a real newspaper for inspiration. Then provide examples of how they might create each section, based on a

nonfiction book you've read together. For example, a newspaper on a book about the Wright brothers might include:

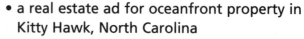

- a top story about their first flight
- a help wanted ad for a job at a bike shop
- a real estate ad for oceanfront property in Kitty Hawk, North Carolina
- a letter to the editor explaining the importance of the Wright brothers' accomplishment
- a cartoon showing surprised birds watching the first human flight
- an ad for the trade fair in St. Louis, where the first successful pilot was rewarded

Assembly: Make double-sided copies of the booklet pages. Have students fold along the dotted lines and nest the pages in numerical order. Staple along the left edge.

Ask the Expert

pages 61–64 • Nonfiction

In this lift-the-flap booklet, students imagine they are experts on their books and answer a series of questions. The last question is left blank for students to fill in and answer. Direct students to fold open the flaps and write their responses on the lines.

Assembly: Make double-sided copies of the booklet pages. Fold each page in half along the dotted line. Cut along the solid lines to create flaps. Place the pages back to back with the flaps facing out, as shown, and staple along the top edge.

Imagine that it is your job to write a sequel to this book. A sequel is a book that takes place after the first book and tells what happens next. What would happen in your book?

_____

_____

_____

_____

_____

_____

7

Independent Reading Response Booklets Scholastic Teaching Resources

IMAGINE... THAT...

What if you could spend a day with a character from your fictional book? Or write a sequel to it? Use your imagination to answer these and other questions.

My Name: _____

Book Title: _____

Author: _____

Imagine that you were asked to write a new title for the book. What title would you choose and why?

_____

_____

_____

_____

_____

6

Imagine that you could visit the setting of the book for a day. (Remember that setting is time and place.) How would you spend the day?

_____

_____

_____

_____

_____

1

Imagine that you could ask the author a question about the book. What would you ask? How do you think the author would respond?

Question: _____

_____

_____

Answer: _____

_____

_____

5

Imagine that the author asked you to write a new ending for this book. How would you end the story?

_____

_____

_____

_____

_____

2

3

Imagine that you could give a gift to the main character in the story. What would you give and why?

3

Imagine that you could ask a character in the book a question. What would you ask and why? How do you think the character would respond?

Question: _____

_____

Answer: _____

_____

_____

4

A Writing "Ad"venture

An advertisement, or ad, tries to convince you to buy something. An ad can tell about a product (like a toy or cookie) or a service that someone can perform (like fixing your kitchen sink).

Think about the characters in your fictional book.

What products or services might help them solve their problems?

Everybody loves...
Big Boy Cookies
The best cookie in the world!

My Name: _____

Book Title: _____

Author: _____

Character 3

Name: _____

What is this character's problem?

_____

_____

What product or service might help this character?

_____

How?

_____

_____

In the box, draw an ad for the product or service.

Independent Reading Response Booklets Scholastic Teaching Resources

Character 1

Name: _____

What is this character's problem?

_____

_____

How? _____

_____

What product or service might help this character?

_____

_____

In the box, draw an ad for the product or service.

Character 2

Name: _____

What is this character's problem?

_____

_____

How? _____

_____

What product or service might help this character?

_____

_____

In the box, draw an ad for the product or service.

PROBLEM 1

Dear _____,
_____ (your name)

My problem is _____
_____
_____

What should I do?

Signed,
_____
(character's name)

2

Draw your picture in the box.

My Advice Column

My Name: _____

Book Title: _____

Author: _____

ADVICE FOR PROBLEM 2

Dear _____,
(character's name)

You should _____
_____

Signed,
_____
(your name)

5

ADVICE FOR PROBLEM 3

Dear _____,
(character's name)

You should _____
_____

Signed,
_____
(your name)

7

Have you ever read an advice column in a newspaper or magazine? In an advice column, one person writes a letter about a problem that he or she is having. The columnist writes back with ideas on how to solve the problem. Imagine that you are an advice columnist, and the characters in your fictional book are writing to you for help. First, write letters from the characters explaining their problems. Then write the advice you would give them.

1

Dear

_____ ,

(character's name)

You should _____

Signed,

_____

(your name)

3

PROBLEM 2

Dear

My problem is _____

(your name)

What should I do?

Signed,

_____

(character's name)

4

PROBLEM 3

Dear

My problem is _____

(your name)

What should I do?

Signed,

_____

(character's name)

6

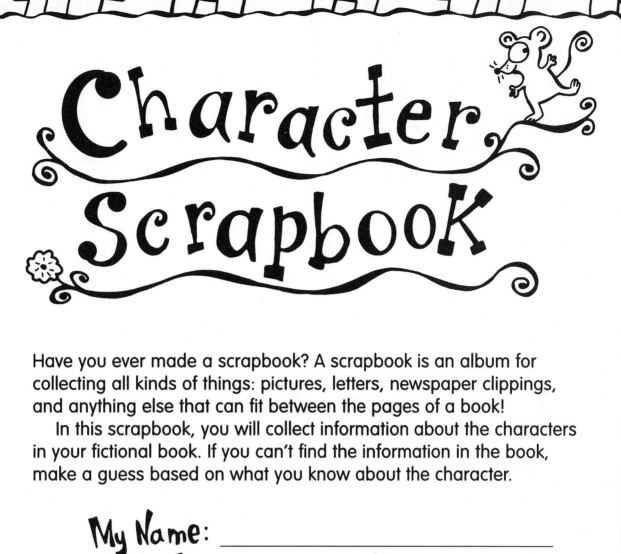

Character Scrapbook

Have you ever made a scrapbook? A scrapbook is an album for collecting all kinds of things: pictures, letters, newspaper clippings, and anything else that can fit between the pages of a book!

In this scrapbook, you will collect information about the characters in your fictional book. If you can't find the information in the book, make a guess based on what you know about the character.

My Name: _____

Book Title: _____

Author: _____

Choose three important characters. Start by writing the characters' names in the boxes below. Then complete one scrapbook page for each character.

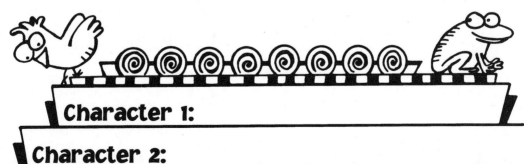

Character 1:

Character 2:

Character 3:

Character

1

Name: _____

In the box, draw a picture of the character.

LIKES   DISLIKES

1.
2.
3.

3 adjectives that describe the character:

1. _____
2. _____
3. _____

Something UNUSUAL about this character is:

_____
_____
_____
_____

This character is important to the story because:

_____
_____
_____
_____
_____

Favorite quotation:

Character 2

In the box, draw a picture of the character.

Name: _____

Something special this character might save in a scrapbook:

_____

Draw a picture and explain why.

Where the character lives:

_____

Favorite activity:

_____

Favorite place:

_____

This character is important to the story because:

_____
_____
_____
_____
_____

Something interesting about this character is:

_____
_____
_____

Favorite quotation:

In the box, draw a picture of the character.

Character 3

Name: _____

Hobbies | Goals for the Future

Favorite quotation:

People this character likes to spend time with:

_____

_____

This character is important to the story because:

_____

_____

_____

Draw a comic strip showing something interesting this character did in the story.

Independent Reading Response Booklets Scholastic Teaching Resources

Which version of the story do you like best? Why?

_____

_____

_____

_____

_____

7

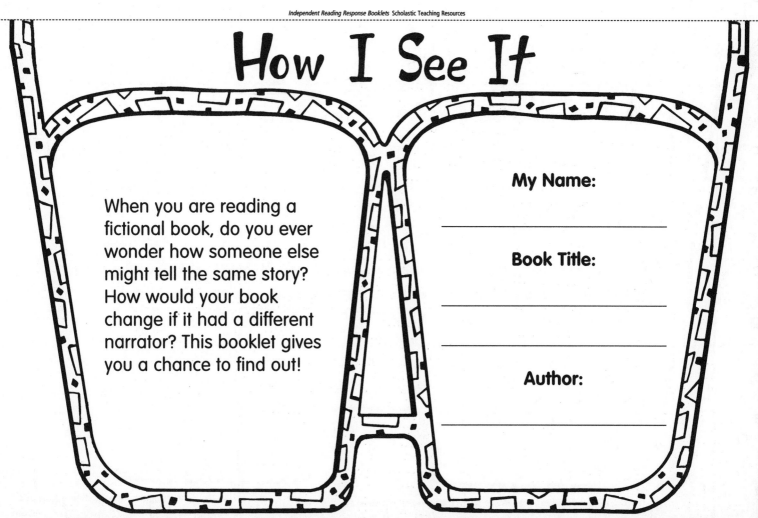

How I See It

When you are reading a fictional book, do you ever wonder how someone else might tell the same story? How would your book change if it had a different narrator? This booklet gives you a chance to find out!

My Name:

_____

Book Title:

_____

_____

Author:

_____

The narrator of a book tells the story from his or her point of view. Sometimes the narrator is one of the characters. Sometimes the narrator is an outside storyteller.

Who is the narrator of your book? Is it one of the characters or an outside storyteller? Give an example that shows who is telling the story.

Narrator: _____

Example: _____

_____

_____

1

What changes about the story when different characters tell it? (Hint: How do the characters feel about the events?) Provide some examples that show how the story is different.

_____

_____

_____

_____

_____

6

This is how the real narrator tells the story (or describes the event).

First, _____

_____

Then, _____

_____

_____

Finally, _____

_____

5

Think about how the book would be different if someone else were telling the story. Then choose two characters from the book to be the new narrators.

Character 1 _____

Character 2 _____

How would these characters tell the events of the story? If your book is long, choose a specific event from the story to retell. (If possible, choose an event that involves both characters.) Then turn the page to write the new versions.

2

This version is how

_____
(character 1)

might tell the story (or describe the event).

First, _____

_____

Then, _____

_____

Finally, _____

_____

3

This version is how _____
(character 2)

might tell the story (or describe the event).

First, _____

_____

Then, _____

_____

Finally, _____

_____

4

My Book of Lists For Fiction

In this booklet, you'll make lists of items that relate to your fictional book: new words, interesting characters, important places, and more.

My Name: _____

Book Title: _____

Author: _____

Independent Reading Response Booklets Scholastic Teaching Resources

---

List five words from the book that were new to you. Look them up in the dictionary. Write the definitions.

Word   **Definition**

1. _____

2. _____

3. _____

4. _____

5. _____

Five Words

Briefly describe four interesting characters in the book.

Name and Description

1.

2.

3.

4.

Four Characters

Briefly describe your three favorite parts of the book.

1.

2.

3.

Three Parts

Independent Reading Response Booklets Scholastic Teaching Resources

Write one book review explaining why you would (or would not) tell others to read this book.

1. _____

One Review

Describe two important places in the book. Explain why each place is important to the story.

1. _____

2. _____

Two Places

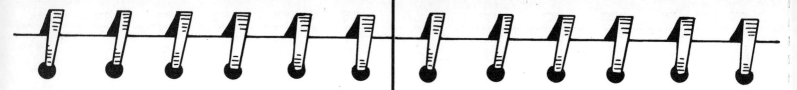

Reporter's Notebook

When writing a news story, reporters answer six big questions:

Who? What? Where? When? How? and **Why?**

Now it's your turn to be a reporter! Dig up some details from your fictional book. Use them to answer the questions in your reporter's notebook.

My Name: _____

Book Title: _____

_____

Author: _____

Who are the important characters in this book? Write a sentence or two describing each character's role in the story.

_____
_____
_____
_____
_____
_____
_____
_____
_____
_____
_____
_____

1

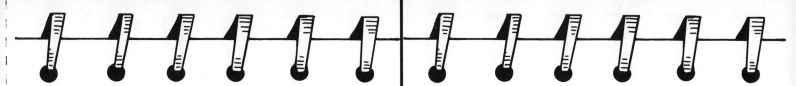

What is the main conflict
(or problem) in the book?

_____

_____

_____

_____

_____

_____

_____

_____

_____

_____

Where does this story take place?
Describe the most important places.
When does the story take place?
Is it in the present, future, or past?

_____

_____

_____

_____

_____

_____

_____

_____

_____

_____

2

3

How is the main conflict (or problem) resolved?

_____

_____

_____

_____

_____

_____

_____

_____

_____

_____

4

Why do you think the author wrote this book? What message did he or she want to get across?

_____

_____

_____

_____

_____

_____

_____

_____

_____

_____

5

The Envelope, Please...

These awards are presented by _____ .
(your name)

Book Title: _____

Author: _____

Congratulations!

You have been selected as an official judge of the Best in Reading Awards. For each category, you will choose three nominees (or possible winners) from your book. Then think carefully about which one deserves to win the award and why.

And the award goes to...	And the award goes to...
And the award goes to...	And the award goes to...

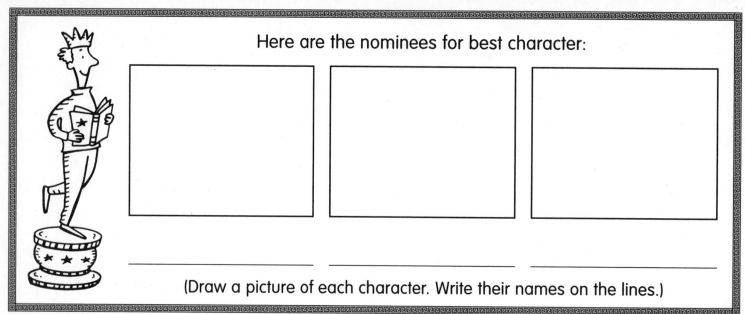

Here are the nominees for best character:

_____   _____   _____

(Draw a picture of each character. Write their names on the lines.)

2A

Best Character

The award for best character goes to

_____!

Explain why this character won. Was this character the most realistic? The most interesting? The character you'd most want as a friend? Include details from the book.

_____

_____

_____

_____

_____

_____

Here are the nominees for most interesting part of the book:

page _____   page _____   page _____

_____   _____   _____

_____   _____   _____

_____   _____   _____

(Write the page numbers. Then briefly describe what happens in each part.)

Most Interesting Part of the Book

The award for most interesting part

of the book goes to page _____!

Explain why this part of the book won. Why was it the most interesting part? What did the author do to make it so interesting? Include details from the book.

_____

_____

_____

_____

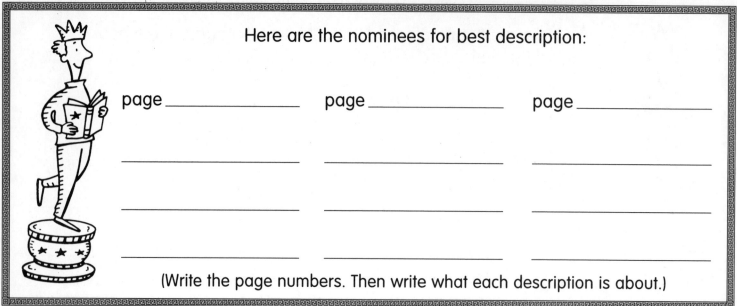

Here are the nominees for best description:

page _____   page _____   page _____

_____   _____   _____

_____   _____   _____

_____   _____   _____

(Write the page numbers. Then write what each description is about.)

Best Description

The award for best description

goes to page _____!

Explain why this description won. What details make it a strong description? What words or phrases stand out? Include examples from the book.

_____

_____

_____

_____

_____

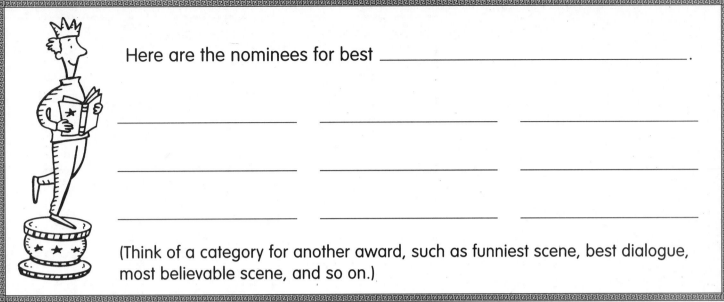

Here are the nominees for best _____.

_____   _____   _____

_____   _____   _____

_____   _____   _____

(Think of a category for another award, such as funniest scene, best dialogue, most believable scene, and so on.)

Best _____

The award for best _____

goes to _____.

Explain your decision. Include examples from the book.

_____

_____

_____

_____

_____

_____

My Book of Lists for Nonfiction

In this booklet, you'll make lists of items that relate to your nonfiction book: new words, interesting facts, questions about the topic, and more.

My Name: _____

Book Title: _____

Author: _____

Independent Reading Response Booklets Scholastic Teaching Resources

---

Five Words

List five words from the book that were new to you. Look them up in the dictionary. Write the definitions.

Word	Definition
1.	
2.	
3.	
4.	
5.	

Describe three helpful photographs, illustrations, charts, maps, or other visual aids from the book. Write the page number of each.

1. _____

_____

page _____

2. _____

_____

page _____

3. _____

_____

page _____

☆ ★ Three Visual Aids ★ ☆

Write four interesting facts that you learned from the book.

1. _____

_____

2. _____

_____

3. _____

_____

4. _____

_____

☆ ★ Four Facts ★ ☆ ★ ☆ ★

Two Questions ✪•★•✪•★•✪

Write two questions you still have about this topic.

1. _____

_____

2. _____

_____

_____

_____

_____

_____

_____

One Review ✪•★•✪•★•✪

Write one book review explaining why you would (or would not) tell others to read this book.

1. _____

_____

_____

_____

_____

_____

_____

_____

_____

_____

Reader's Report Card

Here's your chance to be the teacher and grade your nonfiction book. In this booklet, you will give your book grades for organization, visual aids, writing style, and more. Explain why you gave each grade, using examples from the book.

A Knocked my socks off!

B Good work!

C Got the job done.

D Needs improvement.

F Missed the target.

My Name: _____

Book Title: _____

Author: _____

My Recommendation

I would / would not   (CIRCLE ONE) recommend this book to other readers.

Here's why: _____

_____

_____

_____

_____

_____

_____

Independent Reading Response Booklets Scholastic Teaching Resources

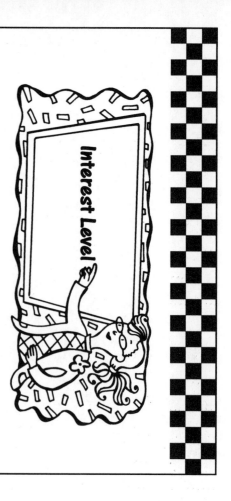

Interest Level

The main ideas in a nonfiction book should keep your interest from start to finish.

I give this book a grade of _____ for interest level.

Here's why:

1

Improvement

There is almost always room for improvement! Here are two things that the author could have done to make this book even better:

1.

2.

6

Organization

A nonfiction book should be well organized. The order of information should make sense and be easy to follow.

I give this book a grade of _____ for organization.

Here's why:

_____

_____

_____

_____

_____

2

Information

A nonfiction book should be informative. That means it should give a lot of information about its topic.

I give this book a grade of _____ for information.

Here's why:

_____

_____

_____

_____

_____

5

Visual Aids

Many nonfiction books use photographs, illustrations, maps, charts, and other visual aids to give information.

I give this book a grade of _____ for visual aids.

Here's why:

_____

_____

_____

_____

_____

3

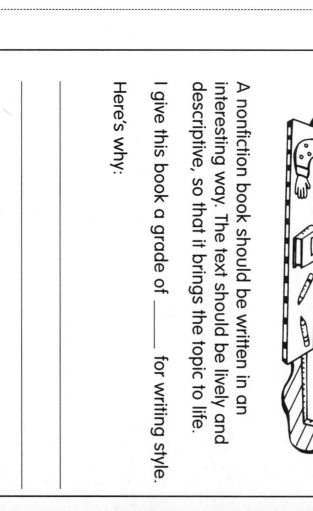

Writing Style

A nonfiction book should be written in an interesting way. The text should be lively and descriptive, so that it brings the topic to life.

I give this book a grade of _____ for writing style.

Here's why:

_____

_____

_____

_____

_____

4

UP, UP, AND AWAY With Nonfiction!

Nonfiction books can take you to all kinds of places! Where did your book take you? In this booklet, you will write about what you saw in your book and what you learned.

My Name: _____

Book Title: _____

Author: _____

Imagine that you are a librarian. Would you buy this book for your library? Use details from the book to support your decision.

_____
_____
_____
_____
_____
_____

7

Choose two important places in your book and write about each.

Place 1: _____

What did you learn about this place?

_____
_____
_____
_____

Fun fact about this place: _____
_____
_____

Do you have any questions you would like to ask the author? Is there anything you'd like to learn more about? Write three questions for the author.

Question 1: _____
_____

Question 2: _____
_____

Question 3: _____
_____

Place 2: _____

What did you learn about this place?

_____
_____
_____

Fun fact about this place: _____

2

What was your favorite part of the book?
Describe what you learned from this part of
the book and why you liked it.

_____
_____
_____
_____

5

Did you read about anyone in your book?
(It could be a person or an animal.)
What did you learn about this person
or animal?

Name of person or animal: _____

I learned _____
_____
_____
_____

3

Brainstorm a new title and cover for this
book. Tell why you chose the title and what
type of illustration you would include.

New title: _____
_____
_____
_____
_____

4

4

In Your Opinion...

An opinion is a statement that tells what someone thinks or feels about something. What do you think is the author's opinion about the topic of this book? What is your opinion?

Author's opinion: _____

_____

_____

_____

_____

Your opinion: _____

_____

_____

_____

_____

7

Nonfiction books can help you learn about a topic that interests you. After reading a nonfiction book, record the information you learned in this booklet.

My Name: _____

Book Title: _____

_____

Author: _____

What's the Main Idea?

What is the main idea of the book? (If the book is long, give the main idea for one part or chapter.)
What details support the main idea?

Main Idea:

_____

_____

_____

Details:

_____

_____

_____

_____

1

It's a Fact!

A fact is a statement that can be proved true. List three facts from this book. How might someone prove that each of these facts is true?

1. _____

_____

_____

2. _____

_____

_____

3. _____

_____

_____

6

Independent Reading Response Booklets Scholastic Teaching Resources

Discover New Words

Find a word from the book that was new to you. What clues in the text helped you understand the word's meaning? Look up the word in the dictionary to check the definition.

Word: _____

Clues: _____

_____

_____

_____

Definition: _____

_____

_____

_____

5

A Picture Is Worth a Thousand Words

Choose an illustration, chart, or other visual aid that helped you understand a part of the book. Describe what it looked like and what it helped you understand.

_____

_____

_____

_____

_____

_____

_____

_____

_____

_____

2

Compare and Contrast

Find two things, people, events, or ideas described in this book. Compare and contrast them. How are they alike? How are they different?

_____

_____

_____

_____

_____

_____

_____

_____

Cause and Effect

A cause is the reason something happens. An effect is the thing that happens. Find an example of cause and effect in the book. Describe it here.

Cause: _____

_____

_____

_____

Effect: _____

_____

_____

_____

_____

Independent Reading Response Booklets Scholastic Teaching Resources

POSTCARDS FROM _____
(main place in your book)

Everyone loves to get a postcard! In this booklet, you'll write three postcards about different things you learned about in your nonfiction book.

My Name: _____
Book Title: _____
Author: _____

Picture of a Person (or Animal)

2

To begin, think about the important things that you read about. Then choose a person, a place, and an object from your book. These will be the subjects of your postcards.

Person _____

(If there were no people in your book, choose an animal or another topic.)

Place _____

Object _____

- On the front of the postcard, draw a picture of your subject.

- On the back, write a message describing the subject. What did you learn about it in the book?

- Then address each postcard to someone who would be interested in its subject. It could be someone you know, someone famous, or someone from history!

1

Message About the Person (or Animal)

Dear _____,

_____

_____

_____

_____

_____

_____

_____

_____

_____,

_____

3

Independent Reading Response Booklets Scholastic Teaching Resources

Picture of a Place

4

Picture of an Object

6

Message About the Place

Dear _____ ,

_____

_____

_____

_____

_____

       _____ ,

       _____

Message About the Object

Dear _____ ,

_____

_____

_____

_____

       _____ ,

       _____

Independent Reading Response Booklets Scholastic Teaching Resources

NONFICTION NEWSPAPER

Congratulations! You've been hired as the editor of a newspaper. Your job is to create a newspaper about the topics in your nonfiction book.

From news stories to comic strips, this newspaper is a place to share the information you learned from your book.

My Name: _____

Book Title: _____

Author: _____

Advertisements

Think of two products or services that relate to your book. Then write an ad for each. Include illustrations.

TODAY'S

Choose a main idea or event in your book. Write a short article that tells all about it. Include supporting details.

1

COMICS

In the space below, draw a cartoon or comic strip that shows an event in your book.

6

TOP STORY

Draw a picture that illustrates part of the article. Write a caption below it. (A caption explains what is happening in the picture.)

2

Letter to the Editor

People write letters to newspapers to express their opinions about different topics. An opinion states what someone feels or thinks about something. Choose a topic or event in your book. Then write a letter that explains your opinion about this topic or event.

Dear Editor,

Sincerely,

_____

5

HELP WANTED

This section of the newspaper advertises jobs that are available. Think of a job that connects to the topic of your book. It can be real or imaginary. Create an ad that describes the job in a few sentences. Draw a picture.

3

Real Estate

This section of the paper advertises homes, offices, and land for sale. Choose one important place in your book and imagine that it is for sale. Create an ad that describes the place in a few sentences. Draw a picture.

4

Ask the Expert

You've been selected as an expert on the nonfiction book you just read. Read the questions and then write the answers beneath the flaps.

My Name: _____

Book Title: _____

Author: _____

Question:

What are three fascinating facts others might not know about this book's topic?

Question:

What is one of the most important places in the book?

Question:

What is the most interesting illustration, chart, or other visual aid in this book? Why?

Question:

What is the most important thing you learned about this book's topic?

The most interesting visual aid is _____

It is interesting because _____ _____ _____

An important place is _____ _____ _____ _____ _____

Fact 1: _____ _____

Fact 2: _____ _____

Fact 3: _____ _____

The most important thing I learned is _____ _____ _____ _____

Question:

If you could ask the author one question about this book's topic, what would it be?

Question:

What is the most interesting part of this book?

Question:

How do you think the author researched this book?

Write your own question here:

_____

_____

_____

_____

The most interesting part

of the book is _____

_____

_____

_____

_____

_____

I would ask the author

_____

_____

_____

_____

_____

I think the author

researched this book by

_____

_____

_____

_____

_____